VOLUME 1

Diary of a LAZY TEEN

Raymond Pender

VOLUME 1
Diary of a
LAZY
TEEN

FKCT[QHC NC\[VGGP
Eqr{tki j v<TC[O QPF RGPFGT

RWDNKUJGF D[<
Rgpf gzr tkpvu
8. Uqrc Qo qrg Uvtv Ovgngtg D1UO
Vgnk2925662; 9; 7.29276567657

Cmtki j vu tgugtxgf CPq rqtvkqp qhvj ku rwdrkecvkqp
o c{ dg wugf y kvj qw vj g gzrtguu y tkvvgp
eqpugpv qhvj g rwdrkuj gtO

DEDICATION

To all lazy teens out there, hopefully, mom would stop bothering us to get up early on Saturday mornings.

ACKNOWLEDGEMENT

First, I personally thank God for giving me the ideas and helping me write this amazing book. He alone deserves the praise.

Then I, thank my family for standing by me through it all. It's not easy y'know. They always stood by my side, helping me, encouraging me; of course, that includes the many times I was shouted at for being too lazy.

And then, I thank my readers and the people who viewed this book and commented ways in which I could make it better.

Love y'all.

SYNOPSIS

Jump into a truthful experience of a super lazy boy. That's me actually. If I got an award for laziness, which I know I will someday, I hope you'll be around to help me collect it.

So, this is like a diary , no, journal . Hope as I share with you my life experience, you learn the good stuffs that I learned, like being lazy. Gosh, it's so comfortable and goooooooood.

Anyway, let me start writing before the laziness takes over. Ciao!

COPYRIGHTS

Now, you are free to copy this as much as you want, cos I'm too lazy to call the cops. But it's gonna sound absurd. Kinda like trying to copy Superman when you have no powers. Laziness is MY superpower and I use it to save people too.......well...... 😌

EDITOR'S NOTE

So, I'm too lazy to check what comes after Copyrights, so I'll just come up with what I can. This is my personal life story.

❌ Don't try any of this stuffs at home!!! ❌⭕⭕

WHATEVER COMES AFTER EDITOR'S NOTE

Now I'm not so rich or handsome. So don't expect to see a cute guy in a big mansion (as I would be putting some pictures, if the laziness does not take over).

Please don't judge me, like if you see me sleeping on a mat, it's cos the bed is so high to get up to, and well.....it is warm on the mat anyway.

ADDITIONAL BONUS

This book also comes with fun facts and quotes from great people. Also packed in it is the first edition of the Raymond's Dictionary.

QUOTE

"LAZY actually means,
Living As Zealous Youths" -
Raymond

So I woke up today, did my devotion and decided to sleep all day. C'mon, it's a lazy Saturday.

I hear people complaining about this lockdown, that it's boring them...I laugh in laziness. Well, my whole life was spent indoors, I'm more of an introvert. [NERD ALERT]

No, no, no! Not that kinda nerd, I'm more like a prince charming.

So I've been told a thousand times that I'm lazy. Well being lazy is not a bad thing y'know, it's like a super power.

It's MY superpower. I haven't begun to save lives yet but I feel it deep down, that there is someone out there, waiting for me to save them (they might have to wait a little long though, it's not my fault that I'm this lazy).

I closed my eyes again and was at the point of sleeping when I heard a familiar angry voice. Mom! *sighs*

You know how in every superhero movie, there's always the big bad villain boss? The one that always tries to harm the hero's precious possessions? Well, that's Mom for you. [M.o.m is actually an acronym for **Menace Opressing Me**, but I'm too lazy to type that in full everytime].

Mom started speaking lot of stuffs all at once, so I made up my mind to pick out the important ones: lazy, irresponsible (kinda sounds like irresistible and ignored the less important ones: wash dishes, sweep, wash clothes etc.

So Mom was actually giving me chores to do. Chores I was supposed to have done yesterday. I tried to explain it to Mom nice and slow. I was a growing young man and needed all the time I could get to improve my speech, hair, muscles and grow other body parts, and the process required you to stay still all day!

Mom really needs to study human (especially young MALE teens) psychology to understand why we do the things we do at times. She however, still insisted on me getting up and doing my chores or she would call Dad [Dangerous And Deadly].

I've seen this scene in a movie once. The villain threatens to destroy the hero with her newly upgraded power, while the hero remains powerless. His power, actually is to stay still and watch life roll by, ability to control channels and television stations with his fancy gadget (the remote), ability to visualize and analyze a screen all day (mobile phone), in one word, LAZINESS.

I finally stood up. What was my first chore

again? Oh yeah, clothes. I got all the buckets ready, cos we don't have a washing machine.....yet. After setting everything and getting the pegs nearby, a thought came in my mind. What if I asked Mom if I could wash first thing tomorrow morning uhn? And so I gave it a try but Mom didn't even turn a listening ear.

I went back to my washing spot and began wondering why we didn't have a washing machine. I'll make sure that when I get a house of my own, I'd get a washing machine first, not a couch, not a bed, but a WM (permit me to call it that, the full name is actually kinda long).

Well after about 30mins/1hour, I decided I was done with washing but Mom made me re-rinse them again about two more times. I hate my clothes.

I scurried back to my lovable mat and cuddled

Mr Snugglesworth. That's my younger brother's teddy.

I later ate breakfast around 1pm. I don't wanna talk about it.

I went back to my bedside and picked up my phone. Then dad started calling me to type something he saw on the internet for him. I discovered that I could copy and paste it, instead of typing it all over from the beginning, pretty smart right?

Dad's work was done in less than a minute and I was back where I truly belonged. My sis *[Seriously Interfering Sibling]* was annoyed that I was lazying around the most and went to report me to Mom. She complained that we needed water, and I had not gotten it. Mom called out my name. No response. Mom called again. Still I kept shut. Then I heard Mom telling my little Sis and little Bro (too lazy to find an acronym for this one) to get the water since the mallam that sold it was directly in front of our house.

My Sis shouted my name and wanted to come and tell me that Mom was calling me but Mom didn't allow it. Hurrah!

Dad later told me to take the soya beans to grind. I went to the store and discovered that their grinder could not really grind it as a result of a problem with their machine. Things are working in my favor. I told Dad and he said maybe tomorrow I'll try another place. With all the troubles I encountered today, don't be surprised if in the future, you see a lotta "Justice For Raymond" placards around.

JUSTICE FOR RAYMOND

QUOTE

"He who says hardwork is the key to happiness has never tasted laziness" - Raymond

June 7

I'm sorry, I was supposed to write a whole lotta things today but..................

QUOTE

"Wanna get a job done in the
very quickest way
possible? Hire a lazy
person" - Raymond

Ah. Woke up today around 9:49am. I said a short prayer and picked up my phone
Then I remembered I had not eaten. I quickly made myself breakfast and told my younger ones to sort themselves out.

Breakfast was real nice. After eating breakfast, I went to greet dad. Mom had gone to school before I woke up.

I really don't understand schools. Must they always open? Even during this lockdown?! If I was a teacher, I would rather stay at home and do online video classes with my students. I can't be stressing myself y'know.

So today I decided [since it was a Monday] to read a book. I went to my bookshelf and whipped out one of my favorites.

I dunno how long I read cos shortly after, I slept off. But I knew (in my heart) that it wasn't less than three hours
I had to go on an errand so I bathed in dad's bathroom. Our own shower (I don't know why parents don't understand that as the shower pours water on our bodies, our souls are warmed up and our tongues begin to produce sweet notes of vocal symphonies).

Dad later told me to grind that soya beans
 (he didn't forget about it at all). I took a bag
from the kitchen and put the plastic in it. I
then trekked to the market cos no one around
my house had a strong grinder, and plus, the
market was somehow close to our house (like
about 178 footsteps far).

I gave the woman the soya beans and she
started grinding. The noise from the grinding
machine was too loud. I was like that monkey
emoji (but not with a smile on my
face). Everyone was just looking at me
like..........

I needed a place to sit so I went to a nearby
shade. I sat on a stool there and looked
towards the grinding shop, no wonder we had
many deaf people in Nigeria. I could already
feel my ears twitching.

I wished I had brought my phone, but I was
afraid someone would steal it. Some chickens

came close by to eat some grain pellets on the floor (I don't know why I'm telling you this chicken part, not like you actually care how chickens feel anyway, hmph).

The woman called me and showed the powdery soya to me. I put some in my mouth. Hmm. Soya!

On my way back, I saw some rams on the road. They were much, I don't really know their total number cos I stopped counting at 5. Now I'm scared of rams, those horns look like sharp objects, and the rams were looking at me in one funny way. Just then, a thought came in my mind (maybe I should go back to the market to see if I had lost anything on the way). So I turned back and headed for the market (cursing the rams under my breath).

I silently prayed for a miracle and it came to me in form of some street boys. They were walking towards the rams and talking loudly. I quickly did a U-turn and started following them. The rams were startled by their noise and shifted a little from the road (as they were spread out across the street before). I hurriedly walked past the street boys when they were passing the last ram. I smiled as I heaved a sigh of relief. The rams didn't get me this time (tho I saw one of the rams looking at me with anger in its face).

I entered my house and showed dad the soya. He nodded after feeling it and told me to keep it. I then went back to my bedside. I picked up a hand fan and started fanning myself. There had been a power cut in the afternoon and it had not been restored. Mom later came home around 6pm. My heart was still beating fast from my earlier encounter with the rams. Deep down, I felt the rams were waiting to set a trap for me. I can't keep running from them forever, but before our next encounter, I would make sure that I'm fully prepared

[RAM – Rapid At Murder]

Fun Fact

Did you know that if you stare in a ram's eye and it stares back, it means it has marked you and will haunt you forever?

If I set my eyes on them......oh.......I'm in no mod to type today, just go.

Arghh, I feel my blood boiling (actually not like boiling water, but y'know, the other type of boiling). Why? Why me? Go away now before I.......

Ok, since your ears are itching for a gist, here's what happened. This stupid NEPA or PHCN hadn't restored power since (actually their new name is PHCN, But I wonder why some people still shout "up NEPA" when they bring the light, ain't it supposed to be "up PHCN"?).

I thought it was general, but something in me was twitching, so I decided to investigate.

I looked in my drawer and picked a shirt, gladly, I had one today to pick from as I had washed earlier this week. I then wore it and set out. Normally, our street shares light with the street down the road (ours is inside inside). I trekked and trekked till I reached the other street. You won't believe it! They did not have power! I was even more furious. I had come outside for nothing.

I looked at how far I had come, there was no way I was going back. After standing for like two minutes (which felt like two days), I started walking back home. I couldn't feel my legs anymore, it was getting wobbly.

 Something in me was telling me to sit on one of those paved sidewalks, but I decided to continue going anyway. I finally reached home and changed into my pyjamas. I lay on my bedside well, not actually groaning, but I was breathing heavily, like real heavy breathings!

Mom wasn't around as she had gone to school hours before I woke up. Gladly, she didn't leave any house chore for me. Dad was too busy pressing his phone to notice me. After some while of *schnoozing, I finally sat up, an idea had ripped through my mind.

¶ Schnoozing (sh-noo-zeen): An act of sleeping with your nose in the air. Raymond's Dictionary 1st Edition

----

What if, I created my own electricity? Like my own power source. I smiled and clapped my fingers, that would be nice. I would be able to charge my phone everytime I wanted. I would show NEPA or PHCN. My family would adore me and not call me lazy anymore. Who knows? They might even stop me from doing any house chore as I would be giving them free power supply unlike the flunctuating one they were paying for.

I didn't know what steps to take so I took up

my phone and decided to Google search it (my phone was about 2% then).

'Easiest way to make electricity without much work.'

I typed, and a bunch of diy's popped up. I picked the first one and watched the tutorial video. It seemed easy so I jotted down the stuffs I was gonna need.

Motor
Battery
Cellotape
Scissors
Copper wire

.

Now, as a science student, I had heard of copper wire before but didn't know how it looked like. This was gonna be a problem. I asked Dad and he gave me a detailed view of it. I went back to my room and brought out the stuffs needed. I didn't really understand

Dad's detailing so I pretty much got lots of wire. I planned on testing them to see which one worked.

Before I started, I decided to have a short nap. I needed the energy y'know. This was a big project and a lotta rest was needed. I woke up shortly after to the sound of my sis washing the plates. Arghh, so noisy. I can't even **rest in peace** anymore.

I looked at the items beside me and decided to start my project. I had not gone long in it when power was restored. (I'm not sure it was me, but someone was screaming, "up NEPA!"

I quickly plugged my phone and switched on the fan. I looked at my unfinished project (more like unstarted project). I smiled and began packing it away. Maybe I would give NEPA/PHCN another chance and not yet make my own form of electricity. I stuffed the items in a box (I discovered it *charges faster when I'm using it Today started as bad, but, like they always say, there's always a light at the end of each tunnel and my light had just shone now.*

QUOTE

"Laziness is equal to
irresponsibility" - Mom

I feel depressed today. Yesterday was an holiday so Mom didn't go to work. Mom came to my room first thing in the morning and, ignoring my greetings, looked inside my laundry basket (sometimes I think that mom has this special power called the clothy sense. This power enables her to know when a cloth was dirty, and Mom was using this power well).

Mom told me that I could not escape it. I was washing today (why does Mom always target my Saturdays for washing?). I tried to tell her that I had washed earlier this week but she told me that I always ate everyday, that I never said that I had eaten earlier this week, so I wouldn't eat again, (but we eat food to live and survive, we don't wash to survive).

So today, I had to wash those silly clothes (again!). And what's more, Mom added more chores for me. I was to sweep the bedroom and the sitting room, and I was to clean the sitting room windows. Now I pretty much know why I

was called Ray [Rarely Appreciated Youth].
The funny thing is, Mom wanted me to do it all
before breakfast, where would I get the
strength to do that?!

I figured out that if I did my chores in the
morning, I would have the afternoon and
evenings all to myself. Mom won't bother me
when she sees me pressing my phone and
relaxing. So I got up right away and got a
broom and dustpan. I swept both rooms and
then went on to clean the windows. My Sis was
tasked with cleaning the bedroom windows
and washing plates. My Bro too was washing
clothes (in fact, he had already done it
before I finally stood up from bed).

After doing two of my chores, mom called me.
There was a lizard in her room and she wanted
me to help kill it, (if later in the future
animals turned on me, well you know who
incited me against them in the first place).

After much chasing of the lizard, I finally killed it. Then we saw another lizard beside the dead one (probably the wife). I easily killed that one as it was not as fast as the first one (probably pregnant). Mom thanked me after I threw them away. She then said I could wash after eating. I ran to the kitchen and cooked macaroni and spag. I started eating but discovered that I needed an egg. Mom said no, refusing outrightly. I panicked. I wasn't gonna eat it plain like that. After much persistent pleas, mum told me to go wash my clothes, as I was bothering her.

I would have asked Dad but he was on an online meeting, via Zoom. I washed and washed and washed till those clothes got clean. Later I snuck back to Mom's room, Dad was done by then, so I asked him if I could have an egg with my meal, seeing we had run out of eggs. He gave me the money and I bought my egg (imagine, 1 egg now costs N40, look what Corona has caused!)

I fried the egg and added it to my food. Yummy but not fair! Everyone had eaten since morning, I was eating my morning food in the afternoon (they were already planning what to eat as lunch then). Mom even said my breakfast was my lunch! Hah! That the next time I would eat was in the evening! I however managed to eat lunch an hour after my breakfast. I was real sneaky. In the night, we ate noodles. I'm happy that I wasn't cheated today. Even though a lot of things made me depressed, with some sunshine and food, I think I'm better now. ҂(°‿°)҂

QUOTE

"It's very hard for a lazy person to make mistakes in life. 1. They don't make rash decisions. 2. They don't make any decisions at all!" - Raymond

You know what? I've been thinking about something lately. Why does the word "mother" rhyme with "murder". This is kinda creepy, y'know, if you really look at it, moms are capable of murder, in so many ways, like giving of house chores for instance. What if someone falls into a coma because of washing too much clothes?

Well let's skip that and talk bout today. Today is fathers' day. Like, really?! Who sets the date on these calendars anyway?! There is a mothers' day, a children's day and now a fathers' day?! I'm not saying we as children are not celebrated, but it should feel more special, not just combining us into a single word "children". There should be brothers' day too y'know.....it's hard work being a bigger brother.

So we ate wheat cereal as breakfast. Not the swallow type, but the liquid one. And guess who had to stay in the kitchen turning it? Yes, this guy, myself.

Our soya is still much so we used it as milk instead of the normal white powdery milk. The thing about soya milk, it's thick; wheat is too. So that combination was too much for me and I had to camp in the toilet all afternoon (a story for another day).

I'm glad to tell you that I bathed early today. I was determined to make today a non-lazy day. I then whipped out a new book as I was done with the 'How Laziness Saved My Life' book. It was now 'Rich Dad, Poor Dad'. Gosh! So interesting and motivating. Somehow, I feel that I'm gonna be very wealthy in future 🙂. I would not work hard like some people....c'mon it's not people who work hard that are rich, y'know, but people who work smart, and what better way to work smart than on your bed in your home with French fries (to keep you focused) beside you?

Lunch was bread and beans. After dropping my plates in the sink for the person that was gonna wash today (whoever that was), I went to check the plans I had written down, and truth be told, I was dissapointed (very dissapointed).

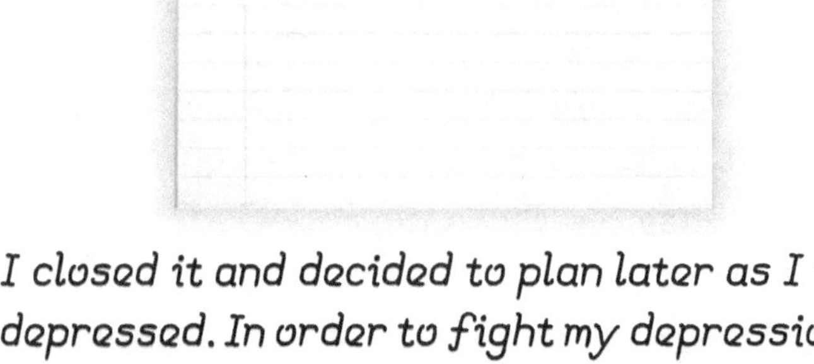

I closed it and decided to plan later as I was depressed. In order to fight my depression, I picked up my phone and started playing this awesome game, Virtual Families 2. Check it out.

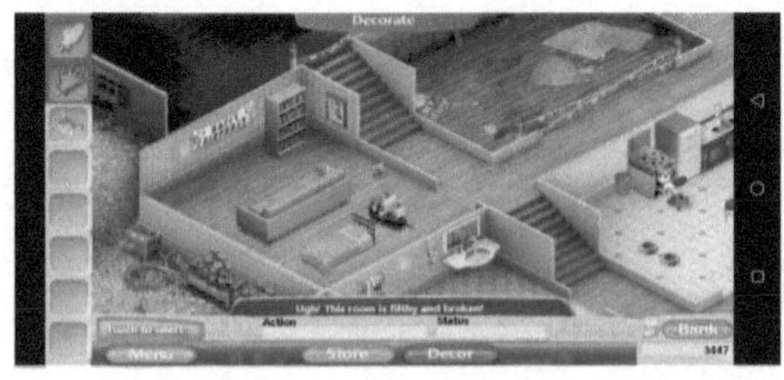

I was supposed to take the trash out today but I forgot, so I quickly did that just as I saw Mom approaching the gate. Mom asked me if I had bathed today and I said yes, but she didn't really believe me and went to ask Dad. I felt offended. Tomorrow, I would not bathe until she comes back so that I shall be justified.

Today was kinda tiring, hard work really takes away one's youthful days. I feel myself getting old. Be warned! Hard work kills!

QUOTE

"The word 'lazy' probably came from a Greek word which means to succeed in an easy way." - Raymond

So today, I came across a new discovery. The person that invented the nose mask was a genius. Now when I wear it, I don't really smell my farts anymore. (As ridiculous as it sounds, it's still a discovery, and I'm waiting for a Nobel prize to be given to me for discovering this amazing fact).

I woke up kinda late today because I slept around 4am. What do you expect? Internet kids don't sleep. My little siblings greeted me and went on with their activities. I answered with a slight groan, hmmhmm.

I washed my face and then greeted Mom. Dad was not around as he had travelled on Friday. Anytime Dad travels, Mom comes to share our room with us.

After greeting Mom, I waltzed back to my bed but Mom said I couldn't go back to sleep. She said we were doing Spring-cleaning today as it was a Saturday. (Why does Mom always

always have something to do on a Saturday, can't we just take a day off housechores? Even God rested on the Sabbath day, which is a Saturday btw)

Now Spring is a beautiful word. When you hear Spring, you imagine flowers, laying in the grass, enjoying the sunset and cool breeze. Cleaning, on the other hand is a very dirty and evil word that involves washing, sweeping and more cleaning. Why would anyone want to mix a beautiful stress-free word with a word that stands for the exact opposite of it?

Well, I still did those chores anyway. Mom never believed that Saturday is a day of rest from all of the week, unlike me, who is a Saturdist. In order to make up for my suffering, I made sure I ate a lot. Lunch was noodles, and since I was a noodle specialist, I deliciously prepared it for them. After cooking, I dished, and....yeah that's right, I wish to continue writing but, my whole body's paining me, I did a whole lot of humongous work today c'mon. And besides, I want to rest and use that time to recuperate and catch up energy, so adios! I just hope Mom lets me have a good rest. There's an adage that says let sleeping dogs (I mean teens) lie.

Fun Facts
The nose mask was invented,
not to fight Corona, but to
fight bad smells that erupts
from good farts.

It's a new monthhhhhhhhh!!!!!! (Well, not new actually cos July always keeps coming every year, but it's the first and only July of this year, kinda like how we celebrate Christmas, celebrate it even when we know it's still gonna come the next year, such a waste of money and time. Why can't we just celebrate these special holidays once?). I don't know if you understand, it sounded a lot better and non-puzzling in my mind. Anyway, let's celebrate.

I woke up and looked to the ceiling...the mosquito net blurred my vision. I wanted to go back to sleep but I had to cook spaghetti for the family. I cooked it and then packed that stupid ol' net. It's so annoying, setting it at night and then packing it the following morning. It's a monotonous house chore (yes, it is a chore). Why can't the mosquitoes even be civilized? Must they always suck blood? Can't they have another form of liquid feeding? I hear tree sap is very very nutritious, so it's best they tried it. Why did

Noah even allow mosquitoes to come with him on the ark???! If it were me, I would have killed em all!

Well, after dismantling the net, I folded my cover cloth and had my devotion. Breakfast wasn't really glamorous, like who would want to eat wheat in the morning?

We had power supply this afternoon so I did some little work on my laptop. That's the only type of work I actually enjoy. Mom's planning on making me wash clothes this Saturday again. I might soon run away (when I have enough money and all the right resources, that is). As I was working on my laptop, Dad came to me and told me to design a flyer for him. I sighed and tried to do it as quickly as possible. Dad! Let me watch my film in peace! Oops, I meant...let me work in peace. Well, you can't judge me. My Sis is always doing like she's my mom. I don't like that! Because she works twice as hard as I do doesn't mean she can use that as an opportunity to call me lazy, especially in front of Mom and Dad. What's she trying to prove? Girls really take after their mothers.

You said what? I don't want to hear 'pim'!

Well, in the evening my Sis continued telling me the story of her book...it's so interesting. Y'all should check it out cos I'm a bad story teller. Yeah I suck at some things, but I know I'm good at some things also. Let me mention a few. I know I'm awesome and smart and intelligent and handsome and friendly and generous and nice and humble and superb and excellent and perfect and beautiful and talented and lazy and courageous and brave and bold and emotional and at times hardworking and awesome (did I say that twice?) and athletic and heavily built and strong and rich (not really rich in material stuffs, but at least I'm rich in proteins). Well, let me stop there before you start thinking

I'm a perfect teen. I'm not perfect, but I'm perfect. You might not really get my theologies as I am a man of many intriguing words and ideas.

Well, all that talking about myself has made me very tired. Wow! It's really hard being myself.

Fun Facts
Studies have found out that 60% of teens in the world are very lazy. 10% are not lazy, but they're not hardworking also. 25% are hardworking, and the remaining 5% work so hard that it's actually a hobby for them.

Arghh! Today is an annoying day, a day that supposed to be removed from the calendar. It's my little Sis' birthday.

She's been ranting on and on about her birthday and it's actually becoming a burden to me. Like, we know it's your birthday, so just shut up already!

So she said that today, she was gonna wear five different clothes. (Like who in the world does that?). Isn't one apparel supposed to be enough for a human per day? I'm suspecting my sis is......(I reserve my comments)

So breakfast was rice and a vegetable soup. You know why I somehow like vegetable? It's got all this little little meat and pomo (treated delicious cow skin, not leather o, please!) floating in it that makes it rather inviting. That's what I look for when eating my vegetables. I enjoyed it and asked for more, but guess what? Right! There was no more! I didn't want to clear my empty plate, in hope that someone would remain part of theirs for me but no one did. People are so selfish!

So we wished my Sis happy birthday. Dad put on his WiFi today so I quickly connected and downloaded lots of stuff. I'm making a game,(name classified) so let's not go there now. But it's a promise that when I finish making it, I'll put up the link for y'all.

Afternoon came quickly. At first Mom didn't want us to eat but after a lot of whining and pleading, she finally relented. Geez! Lunch was bread and egg, but my Sis kept saying she wanted Pepsi, so I had to get it for her. I specially fried the egg (not cos it was her birthday, but because I was hungry and yearned for a well-made omelette). Well, you can guess what I did next, I made a sandwich. (Yummy!)

I washed it down with a drink of water as my

Sis had not started drinking her Pepsi yet. I later collected some of the Pepsi from her when she had almost finished it. My younger siblings should be grateful that I'm not exercising my full rights as Senior of the House. Under Law 49, Section 7 in the house constitution that I made up, Seniors are supposed to issue a 50% food tax on their younger ones, but, me being a good and considerable senior, decided to reduce it to 25%. It's tough for me, but I'm pulling through.

Later towards the evening, I tried to do some push-ups to put my body in shape. I was supposed to do 10 push-ups, but believe me, it's like there was this weight on my back, I could only do two and a half [2½]. In pains, I crawled towards my bedside. How do people who gym everyday do it?

Mom came in and saw me lying on my mat, pressing my phone (my hands had to be busy). Mom told me to get up and sweep the house.

Sadly, I got a broom and a dustpan and started sweeping. Mom was monitoring me as I swept. Mom made me sweep all the corners that I normally hide dirt under (yes, we all have that corner, for some, it's under a rug, under the chair, etc.) Mom put so much pressure on me that I accidentally broke a bottle which was lying on the ground.

I showed Mom immediately. She didn't say anything but just took it away and told me to sweep the glass shards too. Phew! I actually thought Mom was going to bawl out on me.

In the evening, we were supposed to drink wheat again. When Dad asked who was gonna turn it, all eyes fell on me, and I quickly protested. The last four times we ate wheat cereal, I was the one who turned it. And besides, I wanted to write my story. Mom then volunteered to do it so I was sent to get the milk we would use. We later ate the wheat cereal and after family prayers at 8:30pm, I went to continue my relaxation.

Quote
"Anyone bearing the name
'Raymond' was destined for
greatness" – Someone rich.

So I woke up today and greeted Dad. Mom had to go to school again today. However, she had left instructions on what everyone had to do. Dad had come to my room, with much work for me.

Dad wanted me to start the work immediately, I tried to object (I hadn't had breakfast yet!) but Dad didn't answer me. I brought out my laptop and started working. Though my stomach growled at me angrily, I had to subdue it. Soon enough, breakfast, which, as you guessed was wheat cereal, was served. Dad and I went on a short break. Dad ate his cereal quickly and then hurried me to finish mine. (Where's the joy in eating fast? ▢). Because of Dad hurrying me up, I, who normally spent 10/15 minutes tops eating, had to do it in 2 minutes. Way to go Dad! ▢ I just hope I don't choke on my food. Eating was meant to be done slowly.

Because of the frequent power cuts, Dad's

work was finished in the afternoon, just before lunch. Phew! My Sis cooked lunch and came to meet me. She said that Mom had said I should wash my clothes before I ate lunch. I was only allowed to eat breakfast because I was working for dad. After saying that, my Sis went to dish the food.

I looked up to the sky. Does God see all these things happening to me?!

I remembered that we each had our personal angels □. Why doesn't mine help me with my chores, especially washing of my clothes? Well, anyway, I went outside to fetch water from the well as we had not pumped water. I set out my clothes and washed them. They weren't much, just three undies, two tops □ and two trousers.

As I was washing, my Sis walked past me. She reminded me that Mom had said we should be rinsing our clothes five times. It used to be three times for rinsing, but Mom increased it to five times. Imagine. Five times!!! Please, how much does a kidney cost? Will it be enough to buy a washing machine? If it's not, then how much for one kidney plus one liver.

It's better to have one kidney and a washing machine, than to have a complete set of kidneys that only functions to bring energy to wash clothes. Washing clothes is bad for your kidneys. I need to go for a check-up.

I also need all the help I can get. Save A Life, Donate A Washing Machine

*Laziness should be encouraged, not discouraged. It's not easy being lazy y'know. We, lazy teens, suffer much persecution, especially from *anti-lazyists.*

----

*¶ **Anti-lazyists** (antai lay-zee-heests): A person who kicks against laziness and tries to eliminate lazy people.*
Raymond's Dictionary 1st Edition

So, I picked up my dictionary ☐ and checked for the meaning of lazy. I wanted to know how it was defined in the 'English Dictionary'. Here's what I found.

●●●

pronunciation
(IPA): /ley-zi/
adjective (comparative lazier, superlative
laziest)
Unwilling to do work or make an effort;
disinclined to exertion. Get out of bed, you
lazy lout!
Causing idleness; relaxed or leisurely. I love
staying inside and reading on a lazy Sunday.
Sluggish; slow-moving.We strolled along
beside a lazy stream.
Lax:
Droopy: a lazy-eared rabbit
(UK) Wicked; vicious.
synonyms
(unwilling to work) bone-idle, idle, indolent,
slothful, work-shy

●●●

Can you just imagine? They make laziness sound like a bad thing. And they say "scholars" wrote and compiled the dictionary. Hmph! I shall give you the real definition of lazy. So anywhere you see otherwise, just cancel it, scrape it out!

¶ Lazy (lay-zee): A very motivated person who works in a way not understandable to people who love work.
antonym(s): hardwork, hardworker, hardworking
Raymond's Dictionary 1st Edition

Well, I have to go now, I'm so sleepy. I mean like really, really sleepy. My laziness has completely taken over. Feel free to complete this story whichever way you can

THE END
for now...

THE AUTHOR

Raymond Pender, a writer, animator, cartoonist, programmer and a student of Computer Engineering, hails from Delta State, Nigeria. His passion has been his driving force to enable him achieve his goals of reaching out to all and